Microscope

by Sheila Rivera

first step nonfiction

Lerner Publications · Minneapolis

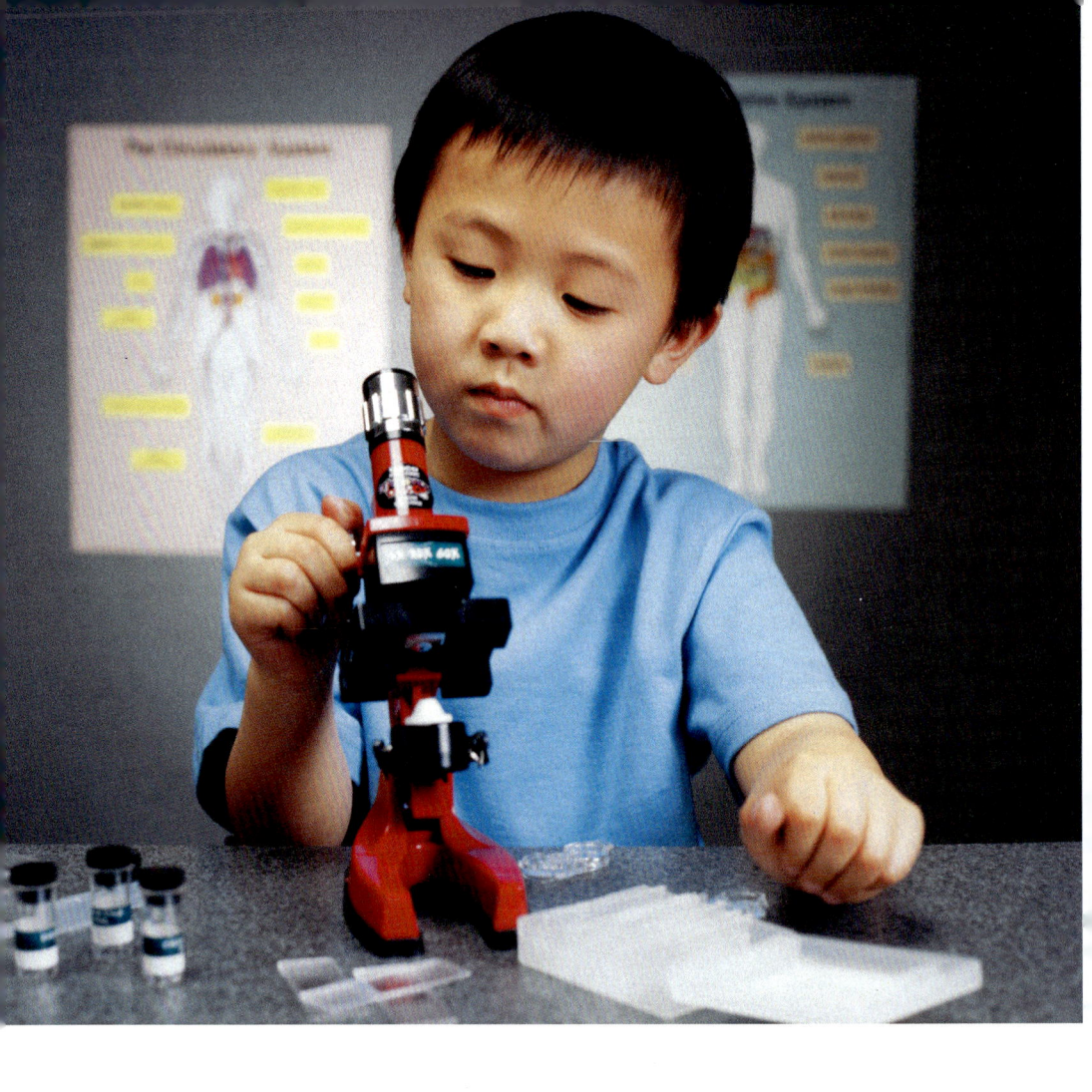

What do you do with
a microscope?

I look at things up close.

I look at a bug.

I look at a leaf.

I look at a feather.

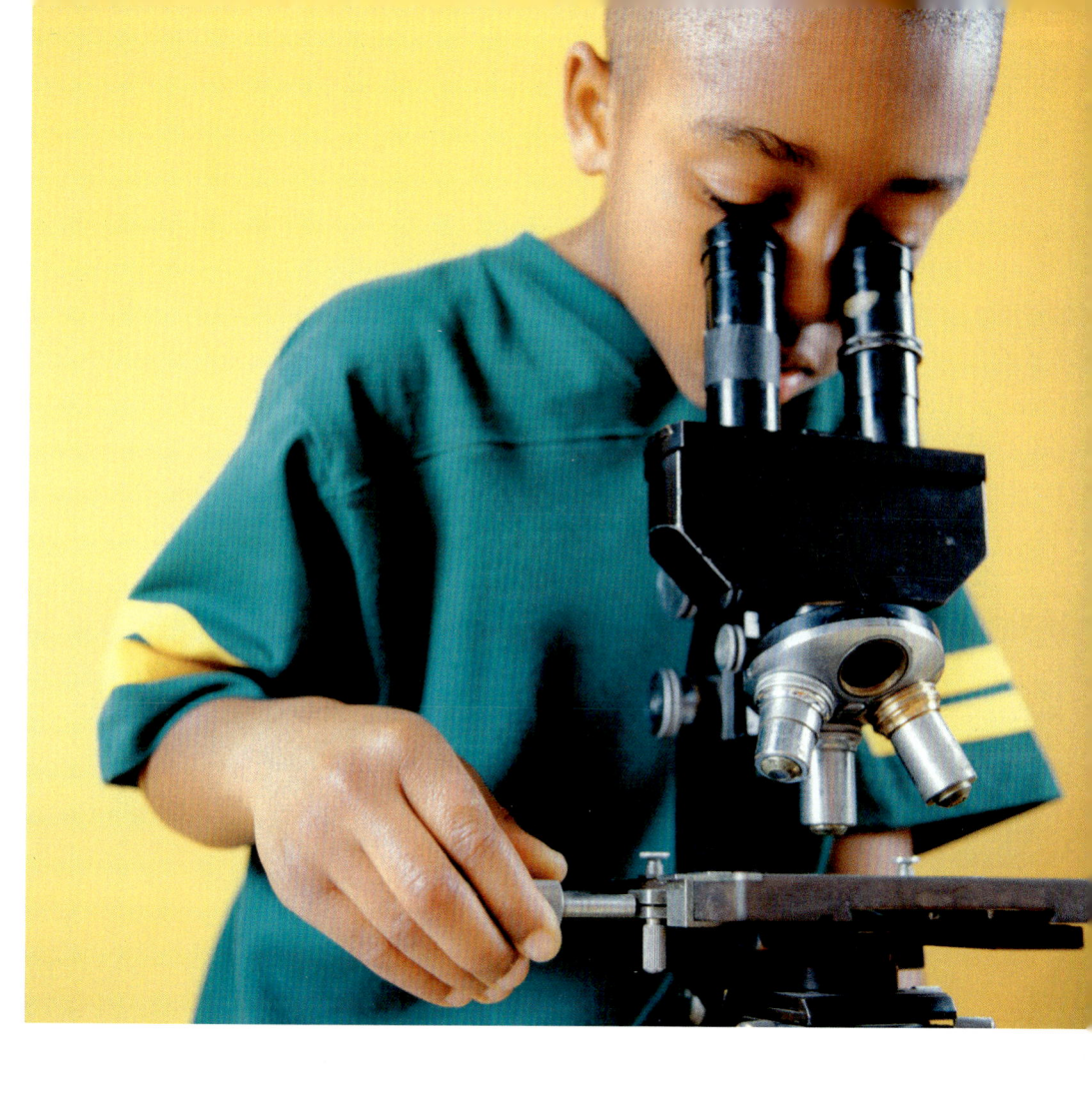

I look at a grain of salt.

Can you use a microscope?